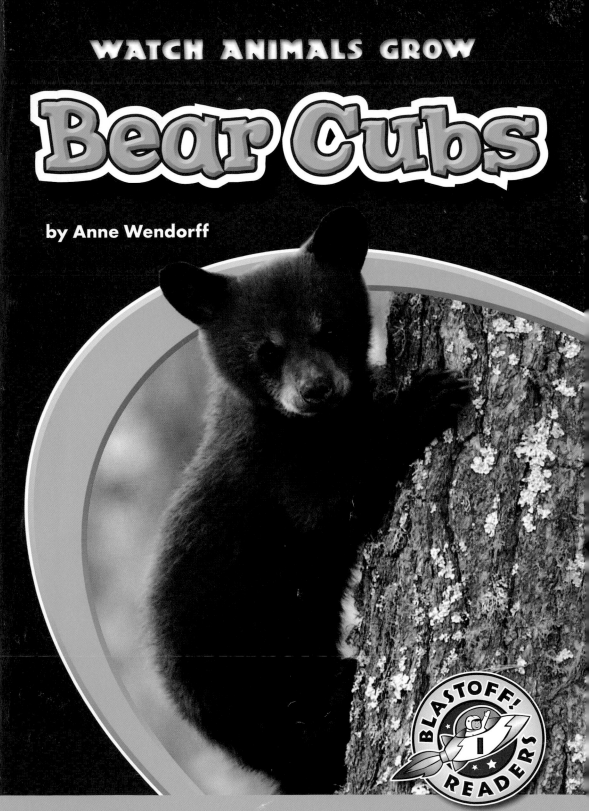

WATCH ANIMALS GROW

Bear Cubs

by Anne Wendorff

BELLWETHER MEDIA · MINNEAPOLIS, MN

BLASTOFF! READERS

Note to Librarians, Teachers, and Parents:

Blastoff! Readers are carefully developed by literacy experts and combine standards-based content with developmentally appropriate text.

Level 1 provides the most support through repetition of high-frequency words, light text, predictable sentence patterns, and strong visual support.

Level 2 offers early readers a bit more challenge through varied simple sentences, increased text load, and less repetition of high-frequency words.

Level 3 advances early-fluent readers toward fluency through increased text and concept load, less reliance on visuals, longer sentences, and more literary language.

Level 4 builds reading stamina by providing more text per page, increased use of punctuation, greater variation in sentence patterns, and increasingly challenging vocabulary.

Level 5 encourages children to move from "learning to read" to "reading to learn" by providing even more text, varied writing styles, and less familiar topics.

Whichever book is right for your reader, Blastoff! Readers are the perfect books to build confidence and encourage a love of reading that will last a lifetime!

This edition first published in 2009 by Bellwether Media, Inc.

No part of this publication may be reproduced in whole or in part without written permission of the publisher. For information regarding permission, write to Bellwether Media, Inc., Attention: Permissions Department, Post Office Box 19349, Minneapolis, MN 55419.

Library of Congress Cataloging-in-Publication Data
Wendorff, Anne.
  Bear cubs / by Anne Wendorff.
    p. cm. – (Blastoff! readers. Watch animals grow)
  Includes bibliographical references and index.
  Summary: "A basic introduction to bear cubs. Developed by literacy experts with simple text and full color photography for students in kindergarten through third grade"–Provided by publisher.
    ISBN-13: 978-1-60014-238-3 (hardcover : alk. paper)
    ISBN-10: 1-60014-238-9 (hardcover : alk. paper)
    1. Bears–Infancy–Juvenile literature. I. Title.

QL737.C27W45 2009
599.78'139–dc22   2008033534

Contents

A mother bear
has cubs.
Bear cubs
are born in
the winter.

Bear cubs are
born blind.
They open
their eyes when
they are six
weeks old.

Bear cubs have
fur when they are
two weeks old.
Their fur keeps
them warm.

Bear cubs live
in a home
called a **den**.

The mother feeds milk to her bear cubs. Milk helps them grow.

Bear cubs grow
teeth to eat
other food.
Their favorite
foods are berries,
honey, and fish.

Bear cubs love to play. They play with other bear cubs.

Bear cubs climb trees to stay safe. Their mother grunts when there is danger.

Bear cubs grow quickly. Soon they are big and strong!

Glossary

den—a cave or hole where some animals give birth and live

fur—hair covering an animal

To Learn More

AT THE LIBRARY

Moody-Luther, Jacqueline. *Black Bear Cub*.
Norwalk, Conn.: Soundprints, 2005.

San Souci, Robert D. *Two Bear Cubs*.
Berkeley, Calif.: Heyday Books, 1997.

Stefoff, Rebecca. *Bears*. New York:
Benchmark Books, 2002.

ON THE WEB

Learning more about bear cubs
is as easy as 1, 2, 3.

1. Go to www.factsurfer.com.

2. Enter "bear cubs" into the search box.

3. Click the "Surf" button and you will see a
   list of related Web sites.

With factsurfer.com, finding more information
is just a click away.

Index

The images in this book are reproduced through the courtesy of: Tony Campbell, front cover; Getty Images, pp. 5, 7, 11; Joe McDonald / Getty Images, p. 9; Suzi Eszterhas / Minden Pictures, p. 13; Daniel J. Cox / Getty Images, p. 15; Karel Broz, p. 17; Ronald Wittek / Age Fotostock, p. 19; Duncan Usher / Alamy, p. 21.